LOT (BIBLE STUDY LEADERS EDITION)

LOT (BIBLE STUDY LEADERS EDITION)

Biblical Characters Series

JAMES G WHITELAW

Swackie Ltd

CONTENTS

1	Opportunity	1
2	Choice	8
3	Consequences	14
4	Salvation	18
5	Faithfulness	24
Author's Note		28

CHAPTER 1

Opportunity

Opportunity – Genesis Ch. 11 v 26 to Ch. 12 v 9
After Terah had lived 70 years, he became the father of Abram, Nahor and Haran.
Abram's Family
This is the account of Terah's family line.
Terah became the father of Abram, Nahor and Haran. And Haran became the father of Lot. While his father Terah was still alive, Haran died in Ur of the Chaldeans, in the land of his birth. Abram and Nahor both married. The name of Abram's wife was Sarai, and the name of Nahor's wife was Milkah; she was the daughter of Haran, the father of both Milkah and Iskah. Now Sarai was childless because she was not able to conceive.
Terah took his son Abram, his grandson Lot son of Haran, and his daughter-in-law Sarai, the wife of his son Abram, and together they set out from Ur of the Chaldeans to go to Canaan. But when they came to Harran, they settled there.
Terah lived 205 years, and he died in Harran.

The Lord had said to Abram, "Go from your country, your people and your father's household to the land I will show you.
"I will make you into a great nation,
and I will bless you;
I will make your name great,
and you will be a blessing.
I will bless those who bless you,
and whoever curses you I will curse;
and all peoples on earth
will be blessed through you."
So Abram went, as the Lord had told him; and Lot went with him. Abram was seventy-five years old when he set out from Harran. He took his wife Sarai, his nephew Lot, all the possessions they had accumulated and the people they had acquired in Harran, and they set out for the land of Canaan, and they arrived there.
Abram traveled through the land as far as the site of the great tree of Moreh at Shechem. At that time the Canaanites were in the land. The Lord appeared to Abram and said, "To your offspring I will give this land." So he built an altar there to the Lord, who had appeared to him.
From there he went on toward the hills east of Bethel and pitched his tent, with Bethel on the west and Ai on the east. There he built an altar to the Lord and called on the name of the Lord.
Then Abram set out and continued toward the Negev.

If you were brought up in a Christian home, then you probably count yourself very fortunate and blessed to have had such a start in life, to have seen and heard, first hand, God at work in your life and the lives of those around you.

That was my position. Having accepted Christ as my saviour at the early age of five, I eagerly listened to teaching and Bible studies in our small assembly and drank it all in. At the age of only nine and a half, I requested baptism, fully understanding what I was asking.

Through until I was fifteen, I attended many services and Bible studies, and my knowledge of the things of God at that age was second to none. Sadly, a change in my circumstances meant that I no longer could attend my Church and I drifted away from the things of God for a few years.

BSLE: Discuss the last few paragraphs and determine your group's background. This may be invaluable as you progress.

However, the word and the knowledge I had gained were ingrained in me, and I have to say, have never left me to this day. I count myself blessed and fortunate to have had the privilege of learning about God at such an early age. What an honour to be taken along to Church from the day I was born and to grow up learning about the Bible from devout and committed men of God

However, my experience, and yours, born into a Christian home, pales into insignificance compared to Lot's experience. Lot had an upbringing and an experience that few have had, save those who walked and talked with Jesus himself.

When we open our Bible on the first page, in the book of Genesis, we read the story of creation, Adam and Eve, then the story of the fall. In chapter five of Genesis, we then have a long genealogy that takes us up to the narrative of Noah and the flood. After a few chapters telling the story of the flood, we return to records of genealogy which take us up to the point where we have started reading here.

It is essential to realise that around two thousand years have elapsed between creation and this point, and apart from Adam and Eve and Noah's family, we have truly little detail about anyone else during this period. Then consider that the remainder of the Bible covers a period of a further two thousand years, and it is clear to see that the twelfth chapter of Genesis is where it all changes and that the real story of the Bible is starting here.

At this point in history, God is doing something completely new. He has had communication with other men. He has favoured other men. He has done great things through other men, but now we come to a point where God is purposefully setting out to make a people for himself. He chooses Abraham(called Abram at that point) to be the father of his own chosen people. The long-held plan of God is swinging into action, which must be one of the most exciting events in the entire Bible.

BSLE: Ensure that your group are all aware that we, as believers, are all now part of Abraham's family.

If we thought we were blessed living in a Christian home, can you begin to see the privileged position Lot was in, being brought up and mentored by his Uncle Abraham, who God had chosen as the father of his people? He was with Abraham when he got the call to leave his country in 'Ur of the Chaldees', which is around the border between Iraq and Iran, and travel thousands of miles, with all their belongings to a place about which they knew nothing.

What a journey. What an adventure. Before and during this journey, Lot would have witnessed Abraham's relationship with God. He knew of the call and observed Abraham's behaviour, how at every place he stopped, he first built an altar to God before he did anything else. He saw first-hand that God was doing something new and wonderful, and he was a part of it. He should have seen the abundance of blessings their small group had, which others did not enjoy. From this realisation, it should be a small step to deduce that God favoured them above all others and that God had chosen them for something unique.

As we read the Bible, we read of privileged people, but indeed Lot was above all, being right at the beginning of God's plans. Was there ever anyone born at such an exciting time, other than around the time of Jesus himself. No. Lot was at the dawn of the history of God's chosen people.

The few chapters of the Bible before this merely introduced God's plans. This is where it all began.

BSLE: Discuss the exciting times in which Lot lived and ask your group if they have ever experienced exciting times in the will of God. Be ready to share your own testimony.

It is worth noting that Lot was not explicitly included in the covenant as he was not one of Abraham's children. However, this did not exclude him from the promise and indeed, as we shall see, did not exclude him from the benefits. Before we continue, let us consider the parallel to our situation. We were not born under the covenant, but we are not excluded. Because we have chosen to accept Christ as our Lord and saviour, we have been grafted into this family of Abraham and partake in the same blessings Abraham enjoyed and the same benefit available to Lot.

In another study, we will look at all the promises made to Abraham and his descendants. They are pretty extraordinary, and when we consider that we, through Christ, are part of Abraham's family and heirs to these promises, genuinely remarkable and greatly exciting.

Lot's father appears to have died when he was very young, and he was raised first by his grandfather, then after he died, became the responsibility of his uncle Abraham. He was part of the movement of God, and both God and Abraham were genuinely concerned about him, as we will see as we study his life later on.

When God blesses us, it results in appreciation and thankfulness, but often, sadly, we see the next generation take it for granted and as their divine right. This seems to be where Lot was and will explain much of what we learn about him. We have seen it in our day also. Families are growing up in a Church environment, blessed by God in every way, but somehow, the younger generation, although continuing to follow along, their hearts are just not in it.

BSLE: Do we see examples of compromise and confusion in our own Churches today?

As we study the character of Lot, we will see a man who believes in God and knows what is right and wrong. When he is amid wickedness, he is aware of it, and it bothers him. He is, however, too weak to turn aside from it and instead tries to keep himself aloof from it while leaving others to live their life as they choose. He certainly does not speak out against wickedness.

Let us examine ourselves. Are we like that? Do we like being in this family? Do we enjoy the benefits only, or are we building altars and calling on the name of God, like Abraham? If we realise the magnitude of the blessings God has bestowed on us, then we must conclude that the depth of love God has for us is way beyond what we could imagine. If we comprehend the depth of his unconditional love for us, how can we fail to build an altar and put our life on it for him?

BSLE: Take a little time to discuss and consider God's unconditional love towards us. Are we willing to put our lives on the altar for his cause?

Imagine the adventure Lot was on, travelling thousands of miles across a desert region to a place of which they knew nothing. We take travel for granted these days. It's so easy. I was working for a period in the Republic of Congo, and I used to leave Cullen in the northeast of Scotland at 3am and land into Pointe Noire, Congo, at 6pm in the evening. Even 100 years ago, this would have been unthinkable and a journey that would have taken weeks and months.

Imagine what it was like in Lot's time, migrating through a desert region and taking everything with you, including staff and livestock. The Bible doesn't tell us how long it took them, but it could have been years. All this time, Lot is witnessing Abraham's relationship with God, learning about God, and experiencing first-hand God's abundant blessings.

If ever there was someone brought up right in the heart of God moving in a big way, it was Lot. The only time in the history of the world, God chose to start building a people of his own. He was mentored personally by a great hero of the faith, blessed beyond anyone else alive at the time with an abundance of every good thing. Surely Lot would follow God wherever he led and not look to the right or the left.

Lot was indeed in a privileged position, living under the direction of the father of nations, the chosen of God, an upright and zealous man. I feel that I have been like that. I grew up under the gospel's sound from my earliest age and was blessed to understand and take in all the fantastic teaching of God's word at a very young age.

How about you? Were you privileged to be brought up in a Christian home and enjoy the teaching of God from an early age? What have you done with that advantage? Have you passed the blessed hope to your children and those whom you have come into contact?

What about your life and work, in general? Does it reflect what God wants for your life? Does it allow you to minister in the way God has called you to, or does it hinder you? In Hebrews 12 v1, The Apostle Paul suggests that we should "lay aside every weight" in our efforts to run a race worthy of the one who laid down his life for us.

Now I am in my 60s, I sometimes look back and consider, did I use that knowledge and learning to the best of my ability, or did I squander it? As we proceed to look at Lot's character, we will find times when he wasted his opportunities, and even times we will ask, 'what was he thinking?'

BSLE: Recap chapter and discuss our privileges in having God's word to study on top of any help or upbringing we may have had. What is our outlook and view on life? What comes first? God's work or our own comfort?

Encourage the group to study the next chapter before meeting again.

CHAPTER 2

Choice

Choice - Genesis Ch. 13 v 1-18

So Abram went up from Egypt to the Negev, with his wife and everything he had, and Lot went with him. Abram had become very wealthy in livestock and in silver and gold.

From the Negev he went from place to place until he came to Bethel, to the place between Bethel and Ai where his tent had been earlier and where he had first built an altar. There Abram called on the name of the Lord.

Now Lot, who was moving about with Abram, also had flocks and herds and tents. But the land could not support them while they stayed together, for their possessions were so great that they were not able to stay together. And quarreling arose between Abram's herders and Lot's. The Canaanites and Perizzites were also living in the land at that time.

So Abram said to Lot, "Let's not have any quarreling between you and me, or between your herders and mine, for we are close relatives. Is not the whole land before you? Let's part company. If you go to the left, I'll go to the right; if you go to the right, I'll go to the left."

Lot looked around and saw that the whole plain of the Jordan toward

Zoar was well watered, like the garden of the Lord, like the land of Egypt. (This was before the Lord destroyed Sodom and Gomorrah.) So Lot chose for himself the whole plain of the Jordan and set out toward the east. The two men parted company: Abram lived in the land of Canaan, while Lot lived among the cities of the plain and pitched his tents near Sodom. Now the people of Sodom were wicked and were sinning greatly against the Lord.

The Lord said to Abram after Lot had parted from him, "Look around from where you are, to the north and south, to the east and west. All the land that you see I will give to you and your offspring forever. I will make your offspring like the dust of the earth, so that if anyone could count the dust, then your offspring could be counted. Go, walk through the length and breadth of the land, for I am giving it to you."

So Abram went to live near the great trees of Mamre at Hebron, where he pitched his tents. There he built an altar to the Lord.

In the last chapter, we considered how privileged Lot was to have grown up under the wing of his uncle Abraham, at a time when God was doing something he had never done before and has never done since. Lot had it all before him, and all he had to do was follow his uncle's example.

This section of the study I have entitled 'Choice'. The immense blessings and benefits that Lot had, having come under the influence of Abraham, continued, and indeed, were so great that they became a problem. Their substance was so great that the land was not big enough to live nearby each other. Abraham suggested that they split up and move their flocks to different areas.

It is fascinating to see the two men's different attitudes in determining which way to turn. Lot looked at the land and saw scrubland and desert to the west. He saw a wide valley, well-watered with good grazing pastures in the other direction. Lot chose the well-watered plain of Jordan with little thought to anything other than the substantial gain this would be for his cattle.

In comparison, Abraham cared not which direction he went. Abraham knew that his success depended not on the world and his surroundings but rather on the God of heaven, who could sustain him just as well in a desert as he could in a lush valley. It is, however, worth taking the time to consider what had transpired in the second half of chapter twelve, which we did not read.

BSLE: What is our attitude to life and God? What would our choice have been? Try to ask questions in the modern context about job and security?

Just after we finished reading the scripture in the last chapter, a famine arose in the land, and Abraham decided to go down into Egypt. God had told him to go to the land of Canaan and settle there. This land was to be his and his descendants land forever. For Abraham to go down into Egypt was a failure, it was a lack of faith and disobedient to God's clear word.

Yes, Abraham made mistakes, wandered away from where God wanted him and landed in trouble at the same time. We all make mistakes. We all fail at some point. We all wander off the path sometimes. The problem is not that we fail but rather, not learning from our mistakes.

At the beginning of this chapter, we see Abraham returning to where it all began in Canaan, to Bethel. He went right back to the place where he had initially built his altar and called on the name of the Lord. Abraham knew he was wrong; he knew he had made a mistake, and it was time to put it right. Lot had been with him the entire time, so had Lot learned a lesson from this episode?

As we discovered in the last section, Lot benefitted greatly, not because he was under the covenant, but rather because he lived under Abraham's influence and protection. Lot had taken this for granted and had given absolutely no thought to what would happen after removing himself from Abraham's circle of influence.

BSLE: Have any of our group learned from others around us, especially their mistakes? Have we made the same mistakes?

This moment is a pivotal moment in Lot's life, and the decision he took showed very clearly that Lot had not learned very much by observing his uncle. All that Lot saw were the benefits that came to him, and he did not appreciate or even question why he had been incredibly blessed.

Very often in life, you will hear Christians offer thanksgiving to God. It is common at times of harvest and such and at other times too. Thanksgiving is in appreciation of the blessings they enjoy and the realisation that they are not merely by chance but come from the hand of the almighty God to his children whom he loves. It is not something we hear of Lot doing, ever.

There will always come a time in our life when we have meaningful choices before us. How do we evaluate these choices, and how are we to decide which course we should take? Sadly, like Lot, we often end up making the wrong choice and going down the wrong road.

When we go down the wrong road, we continue to be blessed. God still loves us, still cares for us, and does not wish that we lose out in any way. However, as we sleepwalk into danger, there are consequences to the choices we make, and if we are to walk into trouble willingly, we should not be surprised if we suffer consequences.

It is imperative in life when big choices present themselves before us that we take time to consider not only the dollars and cents but how they will fit in with God's plans for our lives. We must take time out to pray about important decisions and seek out what God's will is at the time.

BSLE: Do we take all our little mundane things in life to God? Do we consider how all our life's decisions will affect our walk with God?

Lot did not do this, or clearly, his decision would have been different. Common decency also tells us that it would be fitting to tell your uncle that it was his choice to make, as he was the senior member of the household. Lot saw nothing short of profit to influence his answer. The wickedness of the people living in the valley did not concern him, and he could live with that. His life had always been good, so how could that change.

We should acknowledge at this point that Lot would not have condoned the wickedness he saw in the cities of the plains, neither would he have felt comfortable with the depraved behaviour. The problem with Lot is that he did not give this as high a priority as the excellent grazing for his cattle. His thinking would have been that he could get the best grazing in the valley and how the people lived there was not his concern.

There was absolutely nothing wrong with Lot going down into the Jordan valley. It would undoubtedly have been an excellent grazing ground for his herds. At the time, we would be hard-pressed to say that it was a wrong choice. Only with hindsight we can see where the road leads. Would Lot have had a little more than just his herds in mind? Did he perhaps have a hankering after the lifestyle the people of the plain enjoyed?

Sometimes, it is not that there is anything wrong with the things that we do, but instead, we are not afraid of where it will lead. A good thing ceases to be a good thing if there is the potential for it to lead to a bad thing. How often have we started something completely innocent only to find later we had strayed into somewhere we were not comfortable? Do we turn and run, or do we make an excuse, "It's only once, or it is only a minor infraction"?

BSLE: Discuss past mistakes of the group, but be careful and ready to shut it down if it starts to get too personal and revealing. Move any intimate parts to a private discussion with the student involved.

That is how things start, minimal, tiny, almost invisible deviation from what we would consider proper. We justify our actions, and before we know it, we are faced with the same again, perhaps a little deeper this time. Little by little, we let our defences down, justifying our actions the entire time until we suddenly find ourselves in a deep hole.

Lot is at this initial point just now and has to decide. With the absence of the acknowledgement that God held his future and it did not depend on his choice, how would we expect him to choose? Despite all he had seen and heard over the years, Lot had still not arrived at the same conclusion as Abraham, that God could bless him just as well in a desert as he could in a lush valley.

BSLE: Can God bless us in any situation?

This decision that Lot made, not relying on the proper evaluation and conclusion, could only lead to trouble. Although we cannot say precisely how that trouble will manifest itself, we only know that failure to consider God in your life is a recipe for trouble. It is essential to understand that it was not this decision that led Lot astray. Lot was already off track, and this decision was the result.

Lot had, long before this time, prioritised his life as self-first then God if any room was left. It was merely that he had never been put in a position where he had to choose until this point. Now that a choice presented itself, we see for the first time, the real character of Lot appears.

BSLE: Recap and discuss the chapter. Particular emphasis on choice past and future. Reinforce the essential attitude of God first.

Encourage the group to study the next chapter before meeting again.

CHAPTER 3

Consequences

Consequences - Genesis Ch. 14 v 8-16

Then the king of Sodom, the king of Gomorrah, the king of Admah, the king of Zeboyim and the king of Bela (that is, Zoar) marched out and drew up their battle lines in the Valley of Siddim against Kedorlaomer king of Elam, Tidal king of Goyim, Amraphel king of Shinar and Arioch king of Ellasar—four kings against five. Now the Valley of Siddim was full of tar pits, and when the kings of Sodom and Gomorrah fled, some of the men fell into them and the rest fled to the hills. The four kings seized all the goods of Sodom and Gomorrah and all their food; then they went away. They also carried off Abram's nephew Lot and his possessions, since he was living in Sodom.
A man who had escaped came and reported this to Abram the Hebrew. Now Abram was living near the great trees of Mamre the Amorite, a brother of Eshkol and Aner, all of whom were allied with Abram. When Abram heard that his relative had been taken captive, he called out the 318 trained men born in his household and went in pursuit as far as Dan. During the night Abram divided his men to attack them and he routed them, pursuing them as far as Hobah, north of Damascus. He recovered

all the goods and brought back his relative Lot and his possessions, together with the women and the other people.

In the last chapter, we considered whether it was wise to live in the valley close to the wickedness and evil that Lot knew pervaded this area. In this chapter, our fears are justified as we see trouble coming upon Lot and his family. It is not always evident to us what problems may come, but as the old proverb says, 'if you play with fire, you will get burned'. Things can go very well for quite a long time, but it only needs one thing to go wrong for the entire façade to come crumbling down.

If we gamble and take chances, we will get caught out sooner or later, and the consequences are usually significant. This was the case for Lot. I don't know if Lot could foresee this coming, perhaps not, but it is academic. When he chose to live in the heart of wickedness, something would go wrong at some point.

BSLE: Discuss consequences and examine modern-day examples, perhaps within your group.

The Jordan valley is a broad, long valley that stretches for miles in each direction, but in the previous reading, we note that Lot pitched his tent near Sodom. Perhaps Lot just wanted the best grazing for his flocks, but he wanted more than that in time. He had moved away from Abraham as the land could not contain them, but here he was moving closer to a city where land would be at a premium also.

Lot would have noted the people of the valley and their lifestyle. No doubt these people lived a great life. Partying and drinking and all sorts of evil. It is no coincidence that the name Sodom still lives with us to this day with a perverted meaning. Whatever went on in the city, it took the interest of Lot, and he moved nearer to be part of it. We see he has actually moved into the city in this reading.

Sin is attractive, and the only way to deal with it is to flee from it. It is attractive, but it is also dangerous. If you adopt the attitude that you know it is not right but let us look at it anyway, then a look will never be enough. If we even get a glimpse of evil, we must flee from it or else we are doomed, just as Lot was doomed from the moment he moved there.

BSLE: Discuss the attractiveness of sin and admit that it does entice us.

It is interesting to note here that Abraham had no hesitation in jumping into action here. The kings in the valley would have been much more numerous than Abraham's household, and a superior enemy defeated them. Most of us would have considered that and weighed up whether we could do anything at all, and in the face of stiff opposition, would have done nothing. We would have wrung our hands and asked the age-old question, 'What could we have done?"

Where Lot could not resist temptation, Abraham could not resist trusting God. Where Lot could not see how his life could change because it had always been good, Abraham recognised why it was good and was convinced that the God who had looked after him so far would not let him down now.

Abraham must have jumped into action immediately, almost before the messenger had stopped talking, gathered his forces and went on hot pursuit of the enemy who had taken his nephew. It was no real battle with God on his side, and the enemy was no match. The enemy ran, and Abraham pursued them north of Damascus. If we look at the map, we note that Damascus is around one hundred and fifty miles north of where Abraham was settled.

It was no mean feat in those days to cover one hundred and fifty miles and then to recover all the spoils and all the people captured without losing one of his soldiers or the captives. Once again, Abraham's faith had been justified, and his trust in God had been vindicated.

BSLE: Do we have this type of faith where we can answer the call of God in our life without question?

Abraham then returned all the stolen possessions to the kings of the valley, refusing any reward and saved his nephew Lot and his family. You would have thought that Lot may now have taken thought to himself of the consequences of being involved with the men of Sodom.

This story brings home a parallel story where we are estranged and lost and need salvation. Like Lot, there was nothing we could do to remedy our position, but we also had someone who cared greatly for us, enough to go to great lengths to redeem us.

Our position, like Lot, was one of our makings, and we were fully deserving of the fate which awaited us. However, in his loving kindness, God had a plan to rescue us, just as Abraham had. The goal was more arduous and demanded much more than Abraham's plan. Abraham went forth knowing there was a possibility they may not all come back, but God sent his Son, Jesus, into this world to save us, knowing from the start that his life would end on a cruel Roman cross.

It is worth quoting the old hymn here:
Oh! The love that drew salvation's plan.
Oh! The grace that brought it down to man.
Oh! The mighty gulf that God did span.
At Calvary.

Abraham continues his remarkable life after this episode, and some incredible things happen to him. Still, it is around fifteen years later before we take up Lot's story in the next chapter.

BSLE: There is much to discuss in this chapter. There are two sides to the story, Abraham's faith and Lot's failures. As Christians, we will experience both at different points of our lives. The primary discussion here needs to end up on our total dependence and reliance on God.

Encourage the group to study the next chapter and prepare for the next meeting.

CHAPTER 4

Salvation

Salvation - Genesis Ch. 19 v 1-29

The two angels arrived at Sodom in the evening, and Lot was sitting in the gateway of the city. When he saw them, he got up to meet them and bowed down with his face to the ground. "My lords," he said, "please turn aside to your servant's house. You can wash your feet and spend the night and then go on your way early in the morning."

"No," they answered, "we will spend the night in the square."

But he insisted so strongly that they did go with him and entered his house. He prepared a meal for them, baking bread without yeast, and they ate. Before they had gone to bed, all the men from every part of the city of Sodom —both young and old—surrounded the house. They called to Lot, "Where are the men who came to you tonight? Bring them out to us so that we can have sex with them."

Lot went outside to meet them and shut the door behind him and said, "No, my friends. Don't do this wicked thing. Look, I have two daughters who have never slept with a man. Let me bring them out to you, and you can do what you like with them. But don't do anything to these men, for they have come under the protection of my roof."

"Get out of our way," they replied. "This fellow came here as a foreigner, and now he wants to play the judge! We'll treat you worse than them." They kept bringing pressure on Lot and moved forward to break down the door.
But the men inside reached out and pulled Lot back into the house and shut the door. Then they struck the men who were at the door of the house, young and old, with blindness so that they could not find the door.

The two men said to Lot, "Do you have anyone else here—sons-in-law, sons or daughters, or anyone else in the city who belongs to you? Get them out of here, because we are going to destroy this place. The outcry to the Lord against its people is so great that he has sent us to destroy it."
So Lot went out and spoke to his sons-in-law, who were pledged to marry his daughters. He said, "Hurry and get out of this place, because the Lord is about to destroy the city!" But his sons-in-law thought he was joking.
With the coming of dawn, the angels urged Lot, saying, "Hurry! Take your wife and your two daughters who are here, or you will be swept away when the city is punished."
When he hesitated, the men grasped his hand and the hands of his wife and of his two daughters and led them safely out of the city, for the Lord was merciful to them. As soon as they had brought them out, one of them said, "Flee for your lives! Don't look back, and don't stop anywhere in the plain! Flee to the mountains or you will be swept away!"
But Lot said to them, "No, my lords, please! Your servant has found favor in your eyes, and you have shown great kindness to me in sparing my life. But I can't flee to the mountains; this disaster will overtake me, and I'll die. Look, here is a town near enough to run to, and it is small. Let me flee to it—it is very small, isn't it? Then my life will be spared."
He said to him, "Very well, I will grant this request too; I will not overthrow the town you speak of. But flee there quickly, because I cannot do anything until you reach it." (That is why the town was called Zoar.)

By the time Lot reached Zoar, the sun had risen over the land. Then the Lord rained down burning sulfur on Sodom and Gomorrah —from the Lord out of the heavens. Thus he overthrew those cities and the entire plain, destroying all those living in the cities—and also the vegetation in the land. But Lot's wife looked back, and she became a pillar of salt.

Early the next morning Abraham got up and returned to the place where he had stood before the Lord. He looked down toward Sodom and Gomorrah, toward all the land of the plain, and he saw dense smoke rising from the land, like smoke from a furnace.

So when God destroyed the cities of the plain, he remembered Abraham, and he brought Lot out of the catastrophe that overthrew the cities where Lot had lived.

BSLE: This may prove a divisive chapter as topics such as sexuality may mean different things to different people. Try to be sensitive without compromising God's word. Homosexuality is a sin, but emphasise it is a sin in the same way as sex before marriage is.

Much has happened since our last chapter, and there are around fifteen years between events. In the interval, we find things have changed. Lot is no longer merely living in Sodom but is integrated into the city. Lot is living with them, preparing to have his daughters married to occupants of the city, even sitting at the city gate, which would be considered the town council.

Please note this is the first mention of any family Lot has, and we must wonder if his wife was from Sodom, if he had married and had family only since he moved there. Also, we do not know how many daughters Lot had. We know he had two unmarried daughters who fled with him, but there may have been other married daughters who stayed with their husbands and were destroyed.

Yet, despite the integration and slide into corruption, Lot recognised the men who came to the city immediately. He could recognise immediately that these were angels sent from God, and he was afraid. He knew full well that Sodom was an evil place, and it was not safe for these men to spend the night in the square. He insisted that they come to his house.

BSLE: Have any in our group been in a backslidden position and recognise God's influence in their lives?

The inhabitants of Sodom did not recognise who these men were. How could they? They did not know God or his ways. However, they knew there was something different about them, and they want to indulge their corrupt, depraved behaviour by having sex with the men who would be something different for them.

So corrupt and depraved were the men of Sodom that they were not even interested in Lot's two daughters. Women and girls were plenty, and they had a longing for something different. The crowd were very insistent and would have broken down the door had not the two angels of the Lord intervened by striking them all blind.

It is almost unbelievable to us that the entire city was involved in this, but this passage tells us that all the men of the city were there, both old and young. This shows us the depth of depravity to which this city had fallen. It also makes clear God's view of homosexuality. God considers it a sin in the same way as he considers any sex outside of marriage between one man and one woman a sin.

BSLE: We consider our world today to be in total depravity, but this chapter shows us it is not a new phenomenon.

At many places in the Bible, Sodom is cited as an example of depravity and sinfulness. Often, the prophets compare Israel, in her latter days before the captivity, to Sodom. Even today, Sodom is recognised as decadence, and the depraved practice of Sodomy takes its name from the city.

It seems strange that Peter, in 1 Peter 3 v 7, describes Lot as righteous. Lot's life and behaviour seem anything but saintly. We must look to our own position here to understand this. We are sinners, and even after conversion, we continue to sin and often fail God in a big way. We certainly could not claim any righteousness of our own, but our righteousness is granted by the covering of the blood of Jesus.

In the same manner, Lot has no righteousness of his own, but he has come under the covering of his uncle, Abraham, who prayed fervently for him and who pleaded with God for him. We should also note that Lot, although happy to live with it, was not comfortable with the behaviour in Sodom, which indicates the presence of the spirit in him. In the end, Lot is not much different from you and me. A poor sinner made righteous by the covenant and the blood of Christ.

BSLE: Are there things in our lives we are uncomfortable with?

The angels then inform Lot of their true reason for being present here and urge him to get all his things and his people together and flee for his life. This city, however, has such a hold over Lot by now that he is reluctant to escape, and the angels must physically remove him from the city. Once outside the city, they urge Lot to flee to the hills, but even at this stage, Lot is still trying to bargain to stay in the valley.

Why was Lot so reluctant to flee the city? It could well be his possessions and wealth were there, but it may also have been that he had other daughters in the city who would not leave with him. Whatever the reason, Lot resists the Angels all the way, as if he cannot believe that this city is going to be destroyed finally.

BSLE: Why are we always so reluctant to leave the things of the world behind us? Do we have experience of this in our lives?

Lot negotiates to flee to a nearby town, and the angels inform him he must hurry. The angels are forbidden from carrying out their judgment on the valley until Lot and his family reach the town and are safe. Lot's decision saves that entire town, but alas, not his wife, who looks back and is immediately turned into a pillar of salt.

Some Christians live their lives close to the world. They are more involved in the affairs of the world than the affairs of God. Such Christians, like Lot, will be saved, as they cannot lose their salvation, but their lives are totally wasted with nothing to show for their time here on earth. They may have a strong belief in God, but it does not affect anyone around them as their compromise is evident to all. Such Christians will never reach the lost as the lost do not see anything different about them.

At many times in our lives, if we are backslidden, we feel the urging of the spirit on us, just as the angels here urged Lot to flee. Like Lot, we are often reluctant to give up the pleasures of this world, though we know full well the seriousness of the situation. Sometimes we may even be like Lot's wife and return to the depravity, looking back at it longingly and are lost.

BSLE: Discuss this chapter with your group and try to identify which areas of our lives we are too involved with the world and reluctant to give up. Are there things in our lives that impact our witness for Jesus? Do we accept the depravity of others around us? Are we in a position to condemn others, or is that not our place?

Encourage the group to study the next chapter before meeting again.

CHAPTER 5

Faithfulness

Faithfulness - Genesis Ch. 19 v 30-38

Lot and his two daughters left Zoar and settled in the mountains, for he was afraid to stay in Zoar. He and his two daughters lived in a cave. One day the older daughter said to the younger, "Our father is old, and there is no man around here to give us children—as is the custom all over the earth. Let's get our father to drink wine and then sleep with him and preserve our family line through our father."

That night they got their father to drink wine, and the older daughter went in and slept with him. He was not aware of it when she lay down or when she got up.

The next day the older daughter said to the younger, "Last night I slept with my father. Let's get him to drink wine again tonight, and you go in and sleep with him so we can preserve our family line through our father." So they got their father to drink wine that night also, and the younger daughter went in and slept with him. Again he was not aware of it when she lay down or when she got up.

So both of Lot's daughters became pregnant by their father. The older daughter had a son, and she named him Moab; he is the father of the

Moabites of today. The younger daughter also had a son, and she named him Ben-Ammi; he is the father of the Ammonites of today.

You may find it strange that I have entitled this chapter faithfulness. Often, we look at men and describe them as faithful, but in truth, there is no faithfulness compares to the faithfulness of God, and that is what we are looking at in this chapter.

If it were down to us, we would have said Lot made his own bed, and he must lie in it. He made his choice; he must live with the consequences. He was rescued from Sodom, and we owe him nothing more. That, though, is not the way of God. If it were, we would have little hope since we fail him so often by our very nature.

We have looked at the life of Lot, and it has not been a pretty picture. Lot managed to throw away all his advantages in life from a promising start and end up with nothing. Lot made mistake after mistake and spurned every opportunity God gave him.

BSLE: Have we wasted our lives by being far too close to the world? Have we made bad choices? Yet, we are here studying God's word, so God is faithful!

Bearing this in mind, I wish to confess. When I was in my late teens, I thought I would be like King David. I was going to go out there and slay giants. By the time I was thirty, it wasn't going well, I had made some bad choices, and I thought that perhaps I was more like Gideon. I would still do great things for God, but I may test him along the way. I figured I was more akin to Jonah at Forty, still looking to do the Lord's work, but maybe must be dragged, kicking and screaming to do it.

I am now sixty, and I feel God is saying to me, you were wrong. You are more like Lot. That is not a nice thing to hear, but it led me to study Lot's character. If God told me I am more like Lot, then I needed to figure out more about Lot.

The first part of the study was good, just like my own life, but it then developed from bad to worse as his life progressed. I don't know how old Lot was in this chapter's reading, but he was certainly getting on in life and had grown-up daughters. He was living in a cave, and the strangest tale of our entire study presents itself.

It would seem that growing up in Sodom, the daughters had no moral compass and hatched a plan which leaves us stunned. They did, however, know that Lot would not go along with their proposal and that the only way to pull it off was for them to get him drunk so that he did not know what he was doing.

Here is Lot living in a cave and has lost everything, and we would be forgiven for thinking that God is finished with him, but nothing could be further from the truth. We often struggle to understand how God can be so forgiving, so patient, and so longsuffering with us, and this chapter is a classic example. Here is Lot, who had the best opportunity in the world, the most amazing start in life, but threw it all away in pursuit of everything God hated, yet God still loved him, even if it was only for Abraham's sake. When we examine it further, though, it does not hold up that God's benevolence is only for Abraham's sake. If it were, it would have been enough to save him, but God goes much further than that.

Despite everything that had happened, God had not wholly cast Lot off, and he was not done with him. The story we read is indeed a bizarre tale, but the ending is even stranger and a testament to God's faithfulness. From out of the ashes of destruction, God blesses Lot with two grandsons who become two great nations.

Later on in the Bible, we read of the Ammonites who had become a great nation. We also read of the Moabites in the book of Ruth when Ruth, a Moabitess, becomes the grandmother of King David, Israel's greatest King.

BSLE: Have any in our group experiences of God blessingus, despite our attitude to him? Can we point to blessings in our lives we do not deserve?

Having reached the ripe old age of sixty, I can see a parallel here. I have not found it easy to be a Christian and have often failed God, yet when I look back, even when I have failed him, he has never failed me. All the way, he has been looking out for me, and I am convinced that will not change.

Perhaps for the first time in my life, I have realised that I am nothing in myself, without God on my side, but nothing is too difficult with him. In my past, although I have done some work for God, it was always in the back of my mind it was me achieving these things when the truth was that God was leading me along the paths, providing me with the resources and preparing the ground. Like Lot, I had come to take for granted what the Lord had given me.

Like Lot, I am nearing the end of my life, but I pray that I may yet be granted the same faithfulness shown to Lot and that a great nation of redeemed may be the fruit of labours yet to come.

BSLE: This is the end of the study. Discuss this week's reading and discuss the entire character of Lot. If required, take an extra week to recap the study and discuss further. In light of this week's lesson, the emphasis should be on where we go from here in the light of God's faithfulness.

We do hope this has made a difference in the lives of your group, and we would love to hear how God has used this study to build up his people. Please take the time to let us know how you found the book and any improvements you think should be made to it. Also, please let us know if you have any matters you would like us to pray for.

You can contact us through the website shown on the next page.

Author's Note

Author's Note

This marks the end of the book. If you have enjoyed this book, we would ask you to help us.

1. We would be grateful if you could leave a review of the book on Amazon. These reviews are the lifeblood of my business, and without them, I would have no new customers, and I could no longer write books.
2. I would welcome you to contact us through my author website at www.jamesgwhitelaw.com. I can assure you and I am a real person and do not use a pen name. I will answer any questions you have as soon as I am able.
3. Finally, let your friends know that you read my book and enjoyed it on your social media pages.

Thank you for reading the book.

Scripture quotations taken from The Holy Bible, New International Version® NIV®

Copyright © 1973 1978 1984 2011 by Biblica, Inc.™

Used by permission. All rights reserved worldwide.

www.ingramcontent.com/pod-product-compliance
Lightning Source LLC
Chambersburg PA
CBHW021454080526
44588CB00009B/853